POCKET FUN

DINOSAUR
Activity
Book

ARCTURUS

ARCTURUS

This edition published in 2021 by Arcturus Publishing Limited
26/27 Bickels Yard, 151–153 Bermondsey Street,
London SE1 3HA

Illustrated by: Kate Daubney, Kasia Dudziuk, Amanda
Enright, Jo Moon, Claire Stamper, and Leo Trinidad
Designed by: Duck Egg Blue

ISBN: 978-1-78950-045-5
CH006913NT
Supplier 29, Date 0421, Print run 11684

Printed in China

MEAT-EATING GIANT

Giganotosaurus was a huge dinosaur that lived millions of years before T. rex. Connect the dots to find out what it looked like.

Giganotosaurus: jig-an-OH-toe-SORE-us

FINISH THE PICTURE

Doodle plates along the back of each Stegosaurus,
and add some spikes to their tails.

Stegosaurus: STEG–oh–SORE–us

Use your pens or pencils to complete the scene using the guide below.

5

DRAW A TRICERATOPS

1 First, draw the head and neck frill of the Triceratops.

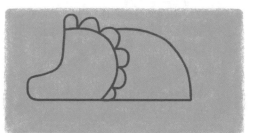

2 Then add this shape for the body.

3 Give your Triceratops four short legs.

4 Add a tail and face. Don't forget to add three sharp horns!

Now you have a try.

Fill this scene with a family of Triceratops!

Complete this roar-some picture of T. rex using the guide below.

Tyrannosaurus rex: ty-RAN-oh-SORE-us REX

DINO BIRD

Hollow bones and a beak-like mouth made Coelophysis similar to a bird. Connect the dots and see for yourself!

Coelophysis: see-loh-FISE-iss

FINISH THE PICTURE

Decorate each Velociraptor with lots of feathers.
They run fast, so be quick!

Velociraptor: veh–LOSS–ee–rap–tuhr

Complete this watery scene using the guide below.

11

THREE-HORNED BEAST

T. rex is on the prowl! Find out which dinosaur it has its eye on by connecting the dots.

Tyrannosaurus rex: ty-RAN-oh-SORE-us REX

13

DINOSAUR DASH

These time explorers have been sent to a prehistoric land. Help them dash back to their time machine before they become dino snacks!

Start here

Exit

FINISH THE PICTURE

Give each Iguanodon spines and spots, and
then draw some ferns for them to munch on.

PREHISTORIC REPTILE

Dimetrodon lived around 280 million years ago.
Connect the dots to see what unusual feature it
had on its back.

Dimetrodon: dy–MET–roh–don

Use the guide below to complete the picture.

17

DRAW A STEGOSAURUS

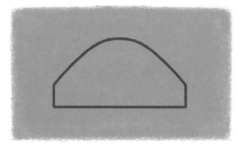

1 Begin by drawing the body of your Stegosaurus.

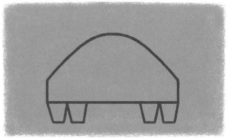

2 Add four short legs.

3 Then draw these shapes for the back plates, tail, and head.

4 Give your Stegosaurus a face and add some sharp spikes to the tail.

Now it's your turn.

Draw a group of Stegosaurus.
Some can be big, and others small.

Complete the scene using the guide below.

20

NIGHT HUNTERS

Troodon had front-facing eyes that helped it spot prey at night. Connect the dots and see for yourself!

Troodon: TROH-oh-don

FINISH THE PICTURE

Doodle lots of dragonflies buzzing
around this prehistoric pond.

Use your pens or pencils to complete the scene using the guide below.

23

DRAW A VELOCIRAPTOR

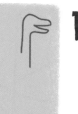

1 First draw the head and neck of your Velociraptor.

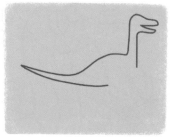

2 Add a body and a long tail.

3 Now draw two legs, feathery arms, and a crest on the head.

4 Finish by adding clawed feet and a face. Remember to add some very sharp teeth!

Now you have a try.

Draw a group of Velociraptors here.

Velociraptor: veh-LOSS-ee-rap-tuhr

FINISH THE PICTURE

Cameroceras was a giant squid-like creature. Draw their long, strong tentacles and plenty of fish swimming in the sea.

Cameroceras: KAM-eh-ro-SEH-ras

HEAD-BANGER!

Pachycephalosaurus had a really thick skull, which it used to ram other dinosaurs in a fight. Connect the dots to bring this one to life!

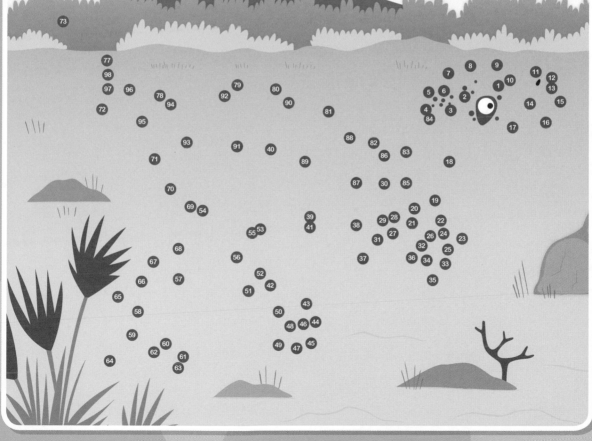

Pachycephalosaurus: pak-ee-SEF-ah-lo-SORE-us

UNDERWATER LIZARD

Discover what Mosasaurus, an enormous sea-dwelling hunter, looked like, as it moved through the ocean searching for prey!

Mosasaurus: MOH-sah-SORE-us

Use the guide below to complete this picture of a defensive Ankylosaurus.

Ankylosaurus: an-KIH-loh-SORE-us

29

DINO DIFFERENCES

Go dinosaur spotting and see if you can track
down ten differences between these scenes.

Use the guide below to complete this sky scene.

32

BIG CHICKEN!

Connect the dots and meet Oviraptor. This dinosaur was covered with feathers and hatched its eggs like a chicken!

Oviraptor: OH-vee-RAP-tuhr

FINISH THE PICTURE

Continue these two trails of dinosaur prints up the page.

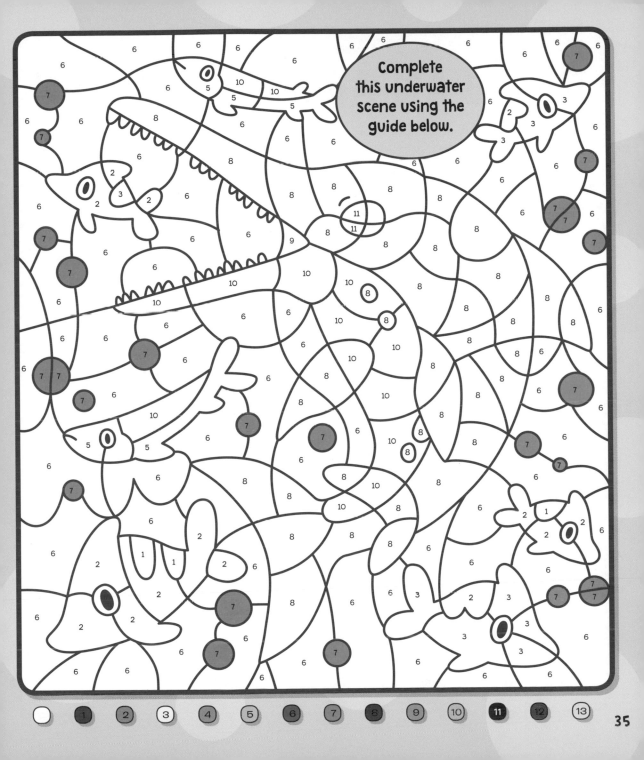

35

DRAW AN ARCHAEOPTERYX

1 Begin with the body of your Archaeopteryx.

2 Add two feathery wings.

3 Draw a head and a long neck. Add some tail feathers and legs.

4 Draw a face like a bird and add two small feet.

Can you draw one here?

Now draw an Archaeopteryx flying in the sky.

Archaeopteryx: ARK-ee-OPT-er-ix

FINISH THE PICTURE

Give each Barosaurus some spines on its neck, back, and tail. Add more spiky leaves to the trees, too!

Barosaurus: BAR-oh-SORE-us

TIME FOR A DIP

Connect the dots to see mighty Stegosaurus wading through the water.

Stegosaurus: STEG–oh–SORE–us

STEP BACK IN TIME

Look carefully to find a baby dinosaur for each of the big dinosaurs. Draw lines to connect them.

Use the guide below to complete this moonlit scene.

41

LIONS OF THE JURASSIC

Connect the dots and meet Allosaurus, a dinosaur
that used to hunt in a pack, like a lion.

Allosaurus: AL-oh-SORE-us

Raaaar!
It's Utahraptor!
Complete the
picture using the
guide below.

1 2 3 4 5 6 7 8 9 10 11 12 13

Utahraptor: YOU-tah-RAP-tuhr

FINISH THE PICTURE

Give T. rex some sharp spines and scaly skin.
You could add some clouds to the sky, too!

Tyrannosaurus rex: ty-RAN-oh-SORE-us REX

GIANT SKULL

Torosaurus had one of the biggest skulls of any land animal!

Torosaurus: TOR-oh-SORE-us

Use the guide below to complete this barren scene.

47

DRAW AN ELASMOSAURUS

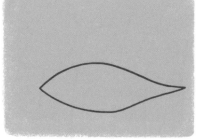

1 Begin by drawing the body of the Elasmosaurus.

2 Add four flippers.

3 Now draw a really long neck and a tiny head.

4 Finish by adding a face and some stripes.

Now it's your turn.

Draw a huge Elasmosaurus coming up for air!

Elasmosaurus: el-LAZZ-moh-SORE-us

LOOK AT MY HEAD!

Dilophosaurus had a double crest on its head,
used to attract mates and frighten enemies.

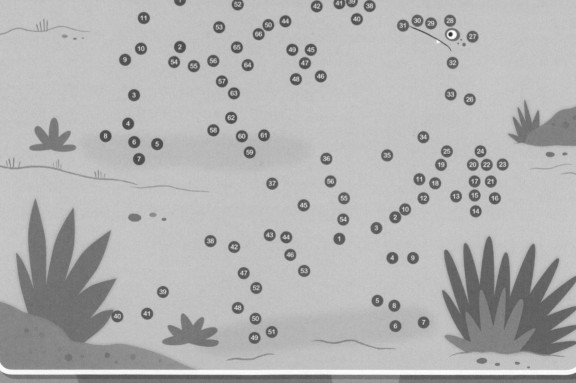

Dilophosaurus: dy-LOFF-oh-SORE-us

SNOW PLACE LIKE HOME

Help the Ice Age children find a safe path over the snow to their frozen cave, without waking the sleepy mammoths.

Home

Start here

FLYING REPTILES

Dimorphodon had sharp teeth, wings, and four grabbing claws.
When on land, it used its wings to walk!

Dimorphodon: dy–MOR–foh–don

Complete this picture of a dino fight using the guide below.

53

DRAW A DEINONYCHUS

1 Deinonychus needs this shape for the head and body.

2 Now add a long tail.

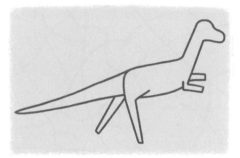

3 Draw two short legs at the front and long, thin legs at the back.

4 Draw a face and add some long claws to the feet.

Can you draw one?

Draw some Deinonychus making footprints in the sand!

Deinonychus: dy-NON-ik-us

Complete the picture using the guide below.

56 ○ ① ② ③ ④ ⑤ ⑥ ⑦ ⑧ ⑨ ⑩ ⑪ ⑫ ⑬

TRUMPET HEAD

Connect the dots to discover Parasaurolophus.
This dinosaur had a bony head crest that it
used for trumpeting!

Parasaurolophus: PA-ra-sore-OL-off-us

FINISH THE PICTURE

Give this sea hunter, Nothosaurus, some scaly skin.
Add lots of bubbles to the water, too!

Nothosaurus: NOH–thoh–SORE–us

Complete this scene of munching Brachiosaurus using the guide below.

Brachiosaurus: BRAH-kee-oh-SORE-us

59

ICE AGE ESCAPADES

Travel through time to the Ice Age. When you get there, spot ten fun differences between the snowy scenes.

Use your pens or pencils to complete the scene using the guide below.

DIG IT UP!

Meet the people who dig up dinosaur bones from millions of years ago. What have they discovered?

FINISH THE PICTURE

These Lambeosaurus are hungry! Doodle lots of tasty leaves and grass for them to munch on.

Lambeosaurus: LAM-bee-oh-SORE-us

Complete the picture using the guide below.

DRAW AN IGUANODON

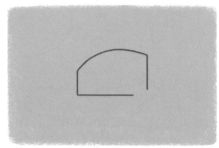

1 First draw the body of your Iguanodon.

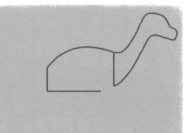

2 Then draw a head and long neck.

3 Now add two back legs.

4 Iguanodon has short front legs, a long tail, and a friendly face.

Can you draw one?

What a hungry group of dinos!
Draw some Iguanodons eating lunch.

Iguanodon: ig-WAH-noh-don

T. rex is on patrol! Complete the picture using the guide below.

68

① ② ③ ④ ⑤ ⑥ ⑦ ⑧ ⑨ ⑩ ⑪ ⑫ ⑬

Tyrannosaurus rex: ty-RAN-oh-SORE-us REX

FINISH THE PICTURE

Kentrosaurus was a prickly character! Draw some back
plates and sharp spikes on the bathing dino.

Kentrosaurus: KEN-tro-SORE-us

FINISH THE PICTURE

Draw more palm trees for the enormous Argentinosaurus to tower over.

Argentinosaurus: AR-juhn-TEE-no-SORE-us

Complete the scene using the guide below.

71

DRAW A MAMMOTH

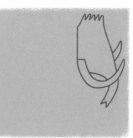

1 First draw the head of your mammoth. Include big tusks and a long trunk.

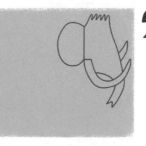

2 Now add a big ear.

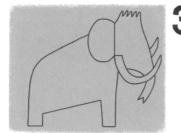

3 Draw the body and two strong legs.

4 Add a tail and the other legs. Give your mammoth an eye and make it brown all over.

Now it's your turn.

Draw a mammoth running away from the cavemen!

LAND OF THE DINOSAURS

Which plant-eater and meat-eater are looking for some lunch?
Connect the dots to find out!

Some dinos lived on land and in the sea! Complete the picture using the guide below.

76

1 2 3 4 5 6 7 8 9 10 11 12 13

HATCHING BABIES

Connect the dots to see who has come out to play!

FINISH THE PICTURE

Give this hungry meat-eater a long tongue, spotted skin, and a toothy grin full of sharp teeth!

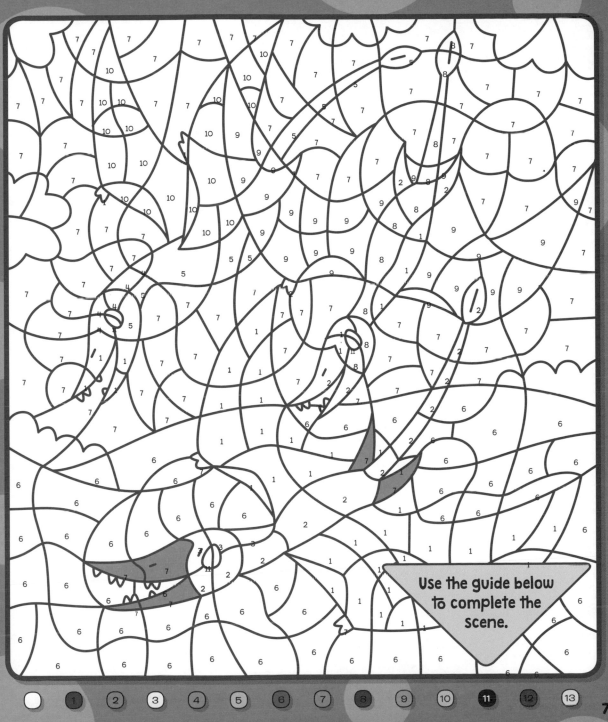

Use the guide below to complete the scene.

① ② ③ ④ ⑤ ⑥ ⑦ ⑧ ⑨ ⑩ ⑪ ⑫ ⑬

79

DRAW A PTERADACTYLUS

1 Draw this shape for the head of the Pteradactylus.

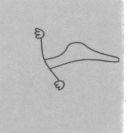

2 Then add a line for the top of the wings, and draw two tiny hands.

3 Now draw some big, sweeping wings.

4 Finish the legs and claws, and then add a face and head crest.

Now you have a try.

Draw some Pteradactylus swooping over the desert!

Pterodactylus: TEH-ro-DACK-tih-lus

Complete this muddy scene using the guide below.

82

FINISH THE PICTURE

Add a head crest and spikes along the back of each Cryolophosaurus. Give them scaly skin too!

Cryolophosaurus: CRY-oh-LOF-oh-SORE-us

GROWING UP

These baby dinosaurs will soon be as big and strong as their parents.

MONSTER OF THE DEEP

Connect the dots to see this Plesiosaurus swimming through the sea, looking for its dinner!

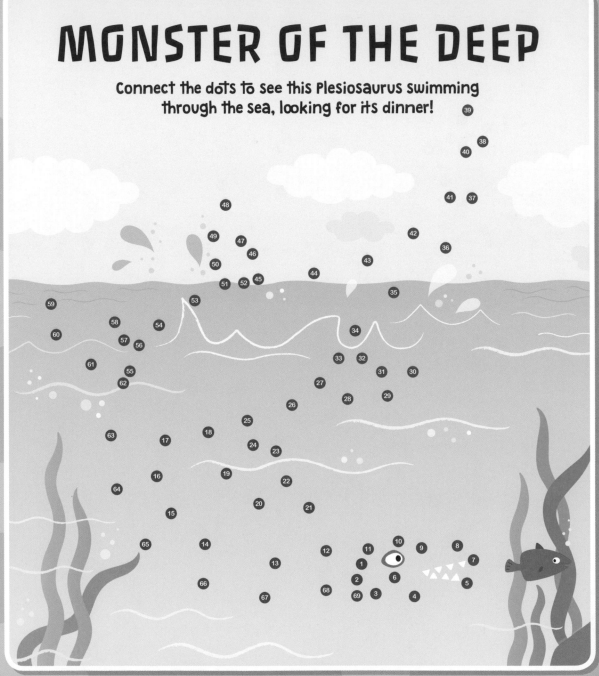

Plesiosaurus: PLEH–zee–oh–SORE–us

Oh no! A forest fire! Complete the scene using the guide below.

87

SPINY LIZARD

Which huge dinosaur, bigger than T. rex, is fishing for lunch?

FINISH THE PICTURE

Draw some bones hidden in the soil, ready to be discovered by dinosaur experts!

ANSWERS

Page 3 MEAT-EATING GIANT

Page 9 DINO BIRD

Page 14 DINOSAUR DASH

Page 5

Page 11

Page 16 PREHISTORIC REPTILE

Page 8

Pages 12-13

Page 17

Page 23

Page 29

Page 20

Page 27 HEAD-BANGER

Pages 30–31 DINO DIFFERENCES

Page 21 NIGHT HUNTERS

Page 28 UNDERWATER LIZARD

Page 32

Page 33 BIG CHICKEN!

Page 40 STEP BACK IN TIME

Page 44

Page 35

Page 41

Page 46 GIANT SKULL

Page 39 TIME FOR A DIP

Pages 42–43 LIONS OF THE JURASSIC

Page 47

Page 52 FLYING REPTILES

Page 57 TRUMPET HEAD

Page 50 LOOK AT MY HEAD!

Page 53

Page 59

Page 51 SNOW PLACE LIKE HOME

Page 56

Pages 60–61 ICE AGE ESCAPADES

Page 62

Page 68

Page 76

Page 63 DIG IT UP!

Page 71

Page 77 HATCHING BABIES

Page 65

Pages 74–75 LAND OF THE DINOSAURS

Page 79

Page 86 MONSTER OF THE DEEP

Page 88 SPINY LIZARD

Page 82

Page 87

Pages 84-85 GROWING UP

We hope you enjoyed all the fun activities!
Before you go, can you find each of us somewhere else in this book?